No Looking Back

Leaving the Past, Prison, and Recidivism Behind

Brenda S. Jackson, PhD

Detroit, Michigan USA

No Looking Back:
Leaving the Past, Prison, and Recidivism Behind
Copyright © 2023 Brenda S. Jackson, PhD

All Scripture quotations, unless otherwise indicated, are taken from the Holy Bible, New International Version®, NIV®. Copyright ©1973, 1978, 1984, 2011 by Biblica, Inc.™ Used by permission of Zondervan. All rights reserved worldwide. www.zondervan.com The "NIV" and "New International Version" are trademarks registered in the United States Patent and Trademark Office by Biblica, Inc.™

All rights reserved. No part of this publication may be reproduced, stored in a retrieval system, or transmitted in any form or by any means – electronic, mechanical, photocopy, recording, or any other – except for brief quotations in printed reviews, without the prior permission of the publisher.

*Priority*ONE Publications
P. O. Box 361332 | Grosse Pointe, MI 48236
E-mail: info@priorityonebooks.com
URL: http://www.priorityonebooks.com

PRINT BOOK
ISBN 13:   978-1-933972-70-1
ISBN 10:   1-933972-70-X

EBOOK
ISBN 13:   978-1-933972-71-8
ISBN 10:   1-933972-71-8

Editing by Patricia Hicks
Cover and Interior design by Christina Dixon

Printed in the United States of America

This Book is dedicated to

DERICK ANTHONY HERBERT

And all others who did not look back.

TABLE OF CONTENTS

INTRODUCTION 7
Recidivism and Backsliding 11
Tools Needed to Plan Change 19
Inner Restraints and Values 29
Transitioning from Prison to Freedom 35
Pressing Toward the Mark 45
BIBLIOGRAPHY 53
APPENDIX 59
About the Author 67

INTRODUCTION
Faith Filled Fear Days
(Going to Prison)

©2009 Brenda Simuel Jackson

My heart pounded, I could hear and feel each beat.

Sweat drops began rolling down my face from fear's heat.

My mind saw danger everywhere my eyes were open to peer,

My hands were shaking, my feet felt heavy, a steady pace hard to keep.

I heard my mouth cry, Lord! I heard my mind say, I walk through the shadow of death, that's no lie, then I felt a calming breeze grab my hand saying I'll walk with you friend.

The pounding in my heart slowed its pace, the sweat drops reduced its running chase.

My Savior in Him, I put my trust and have faith, knowing my fears would diminish in the light of His love and not wanting me my life to waste. I buried my fears in the faithful hands of Him Who is ever near. In faith my fear was challenged, and victory was my cheer.

FOCUSING ON THE FUTURE

©2022 Brenda Simuel Jackson

Out of darkness into God's light, not to return by depending on God's might.

I left the prison walls and was checked in at the half-way parole walls.

With perseverance and prayer, I kept pursuing job opportunities, that would provide personal clearance and care.

The goal is to turn from past ways and never turn back. I cannot make this journey on just strength that I lack.

I won't go back to a life in chains, I will take the minimum wage job to lead me to better gains.

New skills I will obtain that can open up avenues for long lasting gains.

Recidivism and Backsliding
NEVER TURNING BACK

©2022 Brenda Simuel Jackson

The last time my movements will be dictated by someone else's mind. The last time I will be waiting for chow with only 15 minutes to eat, and I am last in line.

I believe my family will be waiting for me on the other side of the fence, I am praying that there will be no obstacles or problems which will force me to stay in lock up on the inmate's bench.

I have my plans in my pocket; I have a place to live, and I have a time set to meet my mentor, and to seek a nearby church. I continue to seek better employment with pay that will meet all my needs here on earth. It sounds easy, but I know it is not, ex-offender is a title that blocks.

I started my spiritual journey when I entered the prison gates. I kept my focus on a future that would truly never be too late. I made up my mind, I would not return to doing prison time. I would stay focused on a future that would keep me spiritually in line. I won't turn back to a life of crime, even if I lose my place to live, and that right employment I cannot find anyone to give.

I have a future of freedom, I have a friend in salvation which is my future, and there is no turning back, my true home is with my Savior in His Kingdom, with Him there is nothing I lack.

LIBERATION

In the book of Exodus, 1:1-13:16, the nation of Israel is freed from 400 years of Egyptian slavery. The Israelites were on their way to land promised to them by Yahweh (God), (Numbers 10:11; Exodus 19:1). "While on the journey, the people complained, murmured, and longed for the delicacies of Egypt. In their heart, they were constantly looking back to Egypt rather than looking forward to a life of liberation from slavery. This looking back led to idolatry and disobedience" (Exodus 16:1-3). The Israelites wandered for 40 years on a journey to freedom which if they had stayed focused, would have taken 11 days. To avoid looking back, Proverbs 4:25-27 says, "Let your eyes look straight ahead, fix your gaze directly before you. Make level paths for your feet and take only ways that are firm. Do not swerve to the right or the left; keep your foot from evil" (NIV, 1985).

When leaving prison, one should use the wisdom of Proverbs to stay focus on not returning.

CHAPTER 1

RECIDIVISM AND BACKSLIDING
(Pigs and Dogs)

2 Peter 2:20-22 (NIV, 1985)

> "If they have escaped the corruption of the world by knowing our Lord and Savior Jesus Christ and are again entangled in it and overcome, they are worse off at the end than they were at the beginning. It would have been better for them not to have known the way of righteousness, than to have known it and then to turn their backs on the sacred command that was passed on to them. Of them the proverbs are true: 'A dog returns to its vomit, and a sow that is washed goes back to her wallowing in the mud'."

For the Israelites in the Old and the New Testaments, dogs were viewed as those who do evil (Richards, Lawrence O. 1984, 308). Pigs were seen as ritually unclean; false teachers were compared to pigs (Richards, 792).

Recidivism of a person is like the action of the dogs and pigs in Proverbs. Recidivism is the tendency of a convicted criminal to repeat or reoffend after already completing their sentence only to go back to their filth.

(Worldpopulationreview.com/state-rankings/recidivism-rates-by-state. Retrieved June 1, 2022, from the World Wide Web).

No Looking Back: Leaving the Past, Prison and Recidivism Behind

In 2004, it was predicted that 2/3 of those released from prison would be in trouble with the law again within three years (Nolan, Pat, "When Prisoners Return", 2004). President Bush stated in his state of the Union address in 2004, 'We know from long experience that if they can't find work, or a home, or help, they are much more likely to commit more crimes and return to prison (Nolan, xii).

In many situations, in 2004 and beyond, inmates were released with little or no money, only the clothes they were wearing, and transportation to a half-way house or the location of their release. Some were homeless at the time of release, and some had family to meet them.

In 2005, about 68% of the 405,000 released prisoners were arrested for a new crime within three years, and 77% were arrested within five years. In 2019, just under 2.1 million people were behind bars in the U.S. Of that, 1.43 million were in federal and state prisons, and 735,000 were in custody in local jails. This is the lowest number since 1995. (Gramlich, John. Pew Research. Retrieved June 1, 2022, from the World Wide Web: https://www.pewresearch.org/fact-tunk/2021/08/16/Americas-incarceration-rate-lowest-since-1995/)

According to the National Institute of Justice, almost 44% of felons released in 2021, were returned to prison within the first year of release (World Population, 2022). For 2022, the highest rate of recidivism, 64.50%, was in the state of Delaware, and the lowest rate 23.40%, was in Virginia. The national average is 43.1% and the median rate is 36%. My state of Michigan's recidivism rate is 28.1%, the lowest it has ever been. Recidivism was based on returning within three to five years to prison for breaking the law or violation of parole (World Population, 2022).

Factors contributing to recidivism are:

1. Social environment
2. Community
3. Circumstances before incarceration
4. Adjusting back into a normal life
5. Reconnecting to family
6. Finding a job

Although there are states where recidivism has decreased, there are states where the rate is higher than in 2004. Yet there are ex-felons who have not returned to prison regardless of the obstacles they faced upon release. What were the factors that helped those to stay focused on starting a new life and staying free. June 28, 2022, Minister Brandon James has been out of prison for 15 years. He is the author of the book, "The Other Side of the Fence". In his new life, he visits prisons and speaks to inmates about their journey in prison, and how that leads to a journey when released from prison. (James, Brandon, Graduation Address, Life Connection Program, Federal Correctional Institution, Milan, Michigan, June 28, 2022.)

He states in his book that he was facing 42 years in prison. He said, "I had a few 24 hours to think about some changes that I had to make before incarceration. On this one, I was going with God, so I totally surrendered to God and His Son." Minister

James spoke to a cohort of inmates who were graduating from an 18-month faith-based program which prepared participants to re-enter society. He stated when he came into the prison and started to serve his time, "I looked at my time as a spiritual journey, not simply as doing time." He established a plan, with specific goals for personal change. Among his goals were:

> "I must love myself
> Respect myself
> Teach myself
> Forgive myself
> Control myself
> Be myself
> Free myself."

He said these goals were a testament of his future. His spiritual journey he started was faith-based in accordance with Matthew 7:13-14:

> "Enter through the narrow gate; for wide is the gate and broad is the road that leads to destruction, and many enter through it. But small is the gate and narrow the road that leads to life and only a few find it." (NIV, 1985)

In prison, Minister James set spiritual goals, that would be maintained on his release. These goals were:

1. Renewed mind (Romans 12:2).
2. Redirection with steps ordered by the Lord (Psalm 37:23-24).

3. Learn how to change and depend on God.
4. Believe in Jesus Christ as this learned behavior.
5. That it will be the last time, I do something.

It has been 15 years since his release, and he has not recidivated. He is a Christian, and to recidivate would be to backslide. Backsliding is returning to questionable habits, losing a sense of God's presence, and being disloyal to God (Richards, 98).

Backsliding is an Old Testament word established on a foundation of a covenantal relationship with God (Richards, 98). Backsliding is a refusal to live by the terms of the covenant, simply disobedience. Backsliding is a rejection of the social and moral requirements of the covenant relationship. Backsliding is a willful choice to turn away from God.

Mrs. T.G. has been out of prison for almost twenty years. She served three short (two years or less) prison terms for non-violent crimes, writing bad checks, using stolen credit cards, and retail fraud. She was interviewed April 20, 2022. She stated that although she confessed Christ at the age of 10, she did not return to Him until her third imprisonment. She stated she married the wrong man between her first and second imprisonment; and had two children, one between each incarceration. It was during her third incarceration that she knew she had to change. She said she was tired of the environment of the prison, and she found herself counseling younger women inmates about changing their lives. She started to turn to her Christian faith, was attending Christian services, and made a commitment not to return once released. She left

No Looking Back: Leaving the Past, Prison and Recidivism Behind

Huron Valley at the age of 55; she now is 75 and has not turned back.

Pastor Tracey Edmonds is the founder and Sr. Pastor of Walk in Truth Ministries, in Lansing, Michigan. Pastor Edmonds was interviewed July 14, 2022. Pastor Edmonds was incarcerated in 1994, and released in 2004, and he has never turned back. He stated, 'I made up my mind before going in, that this would be my last time. I had a God experience' (Edmonds, 2022). He said this was his motivation. His father was a gangster, and he was a drug dealer. After his God experience, his journey in prison was easier than past "bits". He said something happened in his heart. His life changing experience brought a renewing of his mind. He became rooted and grounded, while applying God's truth to his life. He had a ministry in prison and started his ministry when he got out of prison. He said change was hard, and on release peer pressure was the hardest hurdle to resist. He took a minimum wage job, $8.50 an hour. He said that he had never worked a day in his life. He wanted to be able to care for his family, and he knew he was being tested. He said, I could have done better economically; I had not forgotten how to sell drugs, but his aim was to promote the Lord, to continue down a humble path, and to be an example for others. His key scripture was Deuteronomy 30:19:

> "This day I call heaven and earth as witnesses against you that I have set before you life and death, blessings and curses. Now choose life, so that you and your children may live and that you may love the lord your God, listen to His voice,

and hold fast to Him. For the Lord is your life, and He will give you many years in the land He swore to give your fathers, Abraham, Isaac, and Jacob" (NIV, 1985).

He said life was like a garden, and God was trusting him to change his life. He is now helping others not to turn back. He works with the city Mayor and others to reach his goals. He believes he is making a positive impact. He ended the interview with this key: "A key to staying on track is, if you are not doing it in prison, you won't do it when you get out." Everyone who comes to God in prison must be genuine in order to be real with God when released" (Edmonds, 2022).

Chapter 2

TOOLS NEEDED TO PLAN CHANGE

A. Faith and Wisdom

Change is dependent on faith and its application into one's lifestyle. According to Webster's Dictionary (1965), "faith is belief and trust in and loyalty to God; faith is belief in the traditional doctrine of a religion, and belief in something or someone without any proof." Wisdom was defined as "the ability to discern inner qualities and relationships. It is the application of good sense and judgment" (Richards, 1991) combines faith with religion. It states, "wisdom is an approach to life. Wisdom can master life's challenges and be found only in one's relationship with God. Wisdom is expressed in godly living" (p. 629).

In the Bible, the book of Joshua, chapters 3 and 4, three essentials for moving ahead by faith and claiming a new life are illustrated by:

- The Word of Faith
- The Walk of Faith
- The Witness of Faith

(Wiersbe, *The Bible Expository Commentary*, 2002, p.29) The Ark of the Covenant, carried by the Priests during the journey to the Promised land, was an encouragement to the faith of the Israelites. The Ark represented God's presence and His opening up the way to succeed.

(Radmacher, (eds.), *New Illustrated Bible Commentary*, 1999, p. 299) It was through faith applied (wisdom) that Joshua led 1,000,000+ people across the Jordan River on dry ground.

This part of the journey was during a time that the Jordan was at flood stage. By faith, like Moses, Joshua received orders from the Lord. He obeyed and the people successfully crossed over.

To change, self-examination is needed. The examination is by the Word of God. This part of the journey starts, while one is incarcerated. God's Word is like an x-ray, an MRI, or CAT scan that sees the insides of the person and it can assess the condition of the heart. James, author of the Epistle of James, calls the Word of God, 'the perfect law of liberty… because when applied through obedience, one is set free," (James 1:23-25 Amplified Version).

> "For if anyone only listens to the Word without obeying it and being a doer of it, he is like a man who looks carefully at his [own] natural face in the mirror.
>
> For he thoughtfully observes himself, and then goes off and promptly forgets what he was like.
>
> But he who looks carefully into the faultless law, the [law] of liberty, and is faithful to it, and perseveres in looking into it, being not a heedless listener who forgets but an active doer [who obeys], he shall be blessed in his doing (in his) life of obedience."

God's mirror shows the inner person, and the flaws that grooming cannot hide. The wisdom of applying God's word leads to effective service. 1 Corinthians 9:24,27 says, "...Effective service involves self-surrender, self-control and self-sacrifice" (Rydelnik, Michael and Vanlaningham, Michael, 2014, p1788).

B. Mental, Personal, Practical Skills

The wise not only need spiritual knowledge but mental and practical skills are needed to navigate the journey of prison and of society.

On the spiritual journey, the incarcerated should prepare themselves mentally to avoid becoming institutionalized. Preparation includes taking advantage of programs offered by the institution. Such programs include:

- Anger Management
- Parenting
- Gardening
- Dog Training
- Playing an instrument
- Singing in the choir
- Attending worship services.

It is important, wherever possible, to be surrounded by positive people. Through news media, permitted magazines, and family, stay connected with the outside world in order to make it easier, when released, to re-enter society. Having the right attitude helps to focus on the future and not dwell on the past. Sample attitudes include:

- Having realistic expectations about re-entry into society

- Giving yourself permission to accept a minimum wage job
- Promising to forgive yourself when making mistakes
- Practicing being patient
- Joining a group practicing "Mindfulness"
- Knowing that feeling stress at times is natural.

A Getting Ready Release Checkout List is to be prepared and updated regularly. Issues that are likely to be faced are put on the list. These issues may include:

- Substance Abuse
- Lack of money
- Family Issues
- Housing
- Clothing
- Medical needs
- Transportation needs
- Communication devices
- Computer access.

Many institutions provide re-entry services which assist inmates in handling items on the check list (see Appendix I). During incarceration, documents needed on release are misplaced, and licenses have been allowed to expire. Many licenses, such as a driver's license, can be renewed while in prison. There is a monetary cost to renewal. Needed documents are:

1. Social Security Card
2. Birth Certificate

Tools Needed to Plan Change

3. Marriage license
4. Divorce Decree
5. Passport or Green Card
6. Bank account information
7. Military discharge.

From the day you start your prison journey, prepare for the job search that is necessary when released. Opportunities, offered in prison, to earn certificates that validate learned skills are to be taken. Job experiences such as cooking, painting, or knitting can be gained in prison.

Educational program, such as Business Management, are to be taken. Some institution offered College classes, and inmates are eligible for Pell Grants. Volunteer work is available to prison inmates, and such work will help develop skills and build the resume. Maintaining health records will avoid the hassle of getting medical treatment when needed. The prison counselor is a resource to find out what procedures are available for release of health records. Prior to release, requests should be made for a dental exam, eye exam, and physical exam to address any concerns.

Applications for Medicaid, Social Security, and VA benefits can be made prior to release.

C. Transition Plan

In addition to the check list, there is a need for a transition (change) plan. Transition planning is managing the change from the current situation to a future situation. This plan is similar to planning for one's retirement. There will be some overlap between the transition plan and the checklist. There are ten stratagems for the plan (Northwestern University Information Technology, *Project Framework Planning: Transition*, 2020):

1. Ensure the plan identifies who you are and that the plan is for you
2. Layout the tasks and activities needed to take place for a successful plan
3. Indicate the impact on you of this change
4. Identify the risks and contingencies involved in the change
5. Minimize operational and change risks
6. Identify all options that will be available
7. Identify advantages and disadvantages of the plan
8. Estimate time lines and frames for each part of the change
9. Develop appropriate communication channels that may be used
10. Indicate the resources needed to complete the transition.

The content of the plan is based on validated assessments of risks and needs. The content will have appropriate intervention to address the highest areas of criminogenic need. Intervention techniques are shared with members of the case management team. Items on your checklist may be criminogenic such as substance abuse. Transportation must be addressed in the transition plan. Transportation is a key factor in gaining and maintaining employment, attending school, and keeping appointments. The content of the plan includes family issues such as family criminality, domestic violence, sexual offenses, and mental abuse. Low level of personal education may be a criminogenic risk factor. Criminogenic factors are issues causing recidivism. Paying financial obligations are important. Child support debts need to be addressed. The plan's content includes community resources, how to access such resources, and how to use them to meet the needs of the plan.

D. Fears

An action plan to control and overcome fears is the final chapter in planning, and it is very important. This plan undergirds the other plans. This plan is the corner stone of the other plans. This action plan has its focus on God (Clinton & Hawkins, *Biblical Counseling*, AACC Press, 2007).

1. Have a healthy awe of God (Proverbs 1:7)
2. Focus on the character of God, not on the fear. 1 Peter 5:7 says, "Cast all your anxiety on Him, because He cares for you."
3. Focus on the fact that God wants us to trust Him.
4. Focus on giving the fear(s) to God.
5. Reflect on God's strength in Isaiah 26:3 which says, "You will keep in perfect peace him whose mind is steadfast, because he trusts in You."
6. Focus on the fact that God is for us since Romans 8:31 says, "If God is for us, who can be against us?"
7. Know that the Lord guards against anticipated evil for in Psalm 112:7-10 it says, "He will have no fear of bad news; his heart is steadfast, trusting in the Lord. His heart is secure, he will have no fear; in the end he will

look in triumph over his foes. He has scattered abroad His gifts to the poor, His righteousness endures forever; His horn will be lifted high in honor. The wicked man will see and be vexed, he will gnash his teeth and waste away; the longings of the wicked will come to nothing."

8. Know that God is in control of the future, and He is all powerful.
9. Face the fear through trusting God and focusing on your faith in Him.
10. Replace negative thoughts and lies with the truths of the scripture. (Philippians 4:8, "Finally, brothers, whatever is true, whatever is noble, whatever is right, whatever is pure, whatever is lovely, whatever is admirable – if anything is excellent or praiseworthy – think about such things.")
11. Reflect on God's grace which provides and protects.
12. Recognize God's plan for us does not include fear (2 Timothy 1:7, "For God did not give us a spirit of fear, but a spirit of power, of love, and of self-discipline.)
13. Fear is not trusting God. (Psalm 27:1, "The Lord is my light and my salvation whom shall I fear? The Lord is the stronghold of my life, of whom shall I be afraid.")
14. Be willing to honestly analyze the fear – discover the real source. (Proverbs 29:25, "Fear of man will prove a snare, but whoever trusts in the Lord is kept safe.")

Tools Needed to Plan Change
"TO PLAN"

©2022 Brenda Simuel Jackson

A plan is a guide that helps us to keep focused lives.

A plan is a blueprint that helps us to see if our actions are wise.

A plan is reviewed and checked against God's word and promises.

A plan will show us the pitfalls and help us to see poor design decisions.

A plan is not built with bricks of concrete.

A plan is written in pencil or typed in "Word", knowing there is a button called delete.

Proper planning requires prayer, research, and vision.

We must ensure our spiritual journeys include the cornerstone that secures our decisions.

Chapter 3

INNER RESTRAINTS AND VALUES

A prison spiritual journey requires the development of a "moral compass". A moral compass assists in keeping the right focus and going in the right direction. A moral compass is a decision making tool. A moral compass is "a benchmark against which one measures goodness of individual actions and one's life style."("What is a moral compass" www.heartspiritmind.com). The moral compass with the help of one's faith, tells a person which direction to go when decisions involving right or wrong are made.

The setting of one's compass must start with "True North". True north points to what is right. The heart must be in the right place, considering the needs of others before finalizing decisions and taking action ("heartspiritmind.com"). True north points to norms of behavior that follow biblical rules, laws of community, laws of society, and or laws of the country ("True North, ethics sage.com, 2018").

Controlling responses to situations is a result of a strong moral compass. When faltering on the journey, find the strength to do the right thing ("heartspiritmind.com") True North evaluates self-actions:

1. Respecting the rights of others
2. Living up to obligations
3. Evaluating the fairness of actions
4. Treating others equally.

Actions are to be consistent with values such as honesty, empathy, and integrity.

No Looking Back: Leaving the Past, Prison and Recidivism Behind

The concept of True North, right and wrong, is defined by one's belief system and is part of the person's psyche. True North is being ethical. A moral compass creates clear vision of mental processes that point in an ethical direction and guides to making ethical decisions. A moral compass defines character and determines how one will interact with another. Such a character has the following characteristics:

1. Selfless
2. Prideless
3. Honest
4. Truthful
5. Responsible
6. Accountable
7. Self-Disciplined.

Without a moral compass, decisions are made without thinking of the consequences. A morally mature person exercises restraint, curbs desires, and recognizes that material things are not the most important things in life. One's social conscience has a foundation of moral principles.

There are 5 reasons for the need of a moral compass:

1. It grounds person identity by providing consistency.
2. It protects the greater good.
    a. There is a commitment to moral values such as justice.
    b. Others are treated with kindness.
    c. It creates a more inclusive and empowering society.

3. It increases self-confidence.
    a. One feels empowered to act according to conscience.
    b. One feels a sense of integrity, contentment, and focus.

Inner Restraints and Values

4. One develops into a good role model.
    a. One knows who he/she is
    b. A person knows for what they stand
    c. One is able to work through moral dilemma
    d. One is able to foster healthy relationships.

Psalms 121, "A Song of Ascent", was sung by the Israelites, while they were going up to Mount Zion to worship the one and only True God, Yahweh. True North will always point to our Lord. It is a Psalm of assurance with the focus on the Lord and trusting He will watch over the believer. On the way up to Mount Zion, a pilgrim could stumble, get hurt, suffer illness, or even be confronted with robbers, but he never turned back. The faithful people of God looked above and continued on the journey (Wiersbe, 336.) The eyes of the Lord are on the righteous, and His ears are open to their cry.

> Psalm 121: 1-2,7: I lift up my eyes to the Hills where does my help come from? My help comes from the LORD, the Maker of heaven and earth. The Lord will watch over your coming and going both now and forevermore.

Focusing on the future requires moral responsibility. This responsibility is the ability to recognize and respond to circumstances with moral considerations. This is an exercise of free will, and it is required for behavior which is morally responsible. Being responsible is being accountable. Holding someone accountable requires responding to situations that require judgment. There are two responses: moral praise and moral blame. Praise is a response following judgment that one was morally responsible for behavior that is right or good. Blame is judgment that a person was morally responsible for wrong or bad behavior.

No Looking Back: Leaving the Past, Prison and Recidivism Behind

Human action proceeds from knowledge and freedom. "If you take responsibility for yourself, you will develop a hunger to accomplish your dreams (Les Brown). Responsibility is the price of greatness (Winston Churchill). You are responsible for your now. Friedrich Nietzsche stated, "freedom is the will to be responsible to ourselves, and Dietrich Bonhoeffer stated, "actions spring not from thought, but from a readiness to take responsibility." These men were persecuted by Hitler because of their faith. One must understand the limits of their responsibility yet take responsibility in everyday life. The aim is to be your best self.

Integrity is soundness. "It is adherence to values" (Websters, 439). Integrity is being true to one's values and one's self. Keeping commitments is born out of integrity. Failure to take responsibility results in blaming others, blaming circumstances, and being convinced that all is out of control. Staying on the right path requires taking responsibility for personal actions. The role played in one's own life, good and bad, must be acknowledged:

A. Accept the responsibility of being in charge
B. Stop blaming others
C. Stop making excuses
D. Stop bemoaning your situation
E. Follow through on promises and commitments
F. Know what you want in life
G. Take necessary actions
H. Forgive yourself when things go wrong
I. Break bad habits
J. Put it all on paper

Inner Restraints and Values

K. Don't deny your responsibility

("a conscious rethink.com take responsibility")

Values are directives to one's moral compass and are necessary for the spiritual journey in life. "Values provide that inner compass guiding life's direction. ("Mindfulness – Muse', 2020) Values are the standards for judging between right and wrong. Values are statements of what a person wants to be doing with life, and for what a person stands. Values describes how a person wants to behave; values are part of a deep-rooted system of belief. Faith defines core values.

Psalm 119 is a devotional on the Word of God, and it is a source of values that direct us to True North.

PSALMS 119: 1-4

Blessed are they whose ways are blameless, who walk according to the law of the Lord. Blessed are they who keep His statutes and seek Him with all their heart. They do nothing wrong; they walk in His ways. You have laid down precepts that are to be fully obeyed.

CHAPTER 4

TRANSITIONING FROM PRISON TO FREEDOM

Transitioning is passage from one state, stage, or place to another (Webster's, 940). The passage when transitioning from prison to freedom requires focusing on one's future state of being; It is putting the vision of the Transition Plan into action.

Habakkuk 2:1-3

The revelation that God gave the Prophet was for a future time and it was about a future time (Wiersbe, 415). The revelation had an immediate application which was to end Babylonian captivity, a transition to freedom. This vision changed Habakkuk's worrying into worshipping.

> I will stand at my watch and station myself on the ramparts; I will look to see what He will say to me, and what answer I am to give to the complaint. Then the Lord replied: 'Write down the revelation and make it plain on tablets so that a herald may run with it. For the revelation awaits an appointed time; it speaks of the end and will not prove false. Though it linger, wait for it; it will certainly come and will not delay.'

Distractions, such as joblessness, family rejection, or lack of money, can be obstacles that blur one's focus, and take one off the plan.

No Looking Back: Leaving the Past, Prison and Recidivism Behind

Hebrew 12:1-2 says:

> "Therefore since we are surrounded by such a great cloud of witnesses, let us throw off everything that hinders, and the sin that so easily entangles, let us run with perseverance the race marked out for us."

There is help to stay focused. The great cloud of witnesses are believers, who bear witness about the journey, and witness that God will see one through. Listen to those who made it.

This transition passage is part of the on-going spiritual journey, therefore follow Hebrews 12:2-3:

> "Let us fix our eyes on Jesus, the author and perfecter of our faith, who for the joy set before Him <u>endured</u> the cross, scorning its shame, and sat down at the right hand of the throne of God. Consider Him who <u>endured</u> such opposition from sinful men, so that you will not grow weary and lose heart."

Remember rewards are in the future. Some the immediate future, others the distant future. The decision made today will determine future rewards. The passage in Hebrews speaks to perseverance and endurance. Endurance relates to results which are commendable; and they do not discredit one. Negative endurance is activities such as getting back with the old crowd. It is getting off the spiritual journey and abandoning the

Church. It is going against the rules and the authorities. It is losing the way.

How does one endure while on this transition passage?

1. Obtain a mentor or join a support group that will give encouragement and sound advice.
2. Have hope in deliverance that circumstances will change.
3. Maintain your faith precepts and prayer life.
4. Keep a spiritual attitude.
5. Count the obstacles as trials.
6. Seek and receive God's comfort.
7. Encourage others.

Samples of Biblical Endurance

Scriptures	Definitions	Biblical Context	Application
Genesis 33:14	To endure walking	Jacob is meeting Esau after a separation, and he seeks to lead at such a pace that the children will be able to walk.	There is a need for physical endurance; how we walk in this life
Exodus 18:23	To endure is to arise, to confirm, to continue to stand	Moses is being counseled by his father-in-law regarding his need for assistance if he is to endure the strain.	Sometimes help is needed in order to endure.
Psalm 30:5	To endure is to stay.	The temple is being dedicated to the Lord, and the worshippers feel security and seek to praise Him, Struggles are temporary in comparison to God's favor.	We need to stay in God's counsel during struggles. We must remember struggles are temporary, but God's favor is everlasting.

Scriptures	Definitions	Biblical Context	Application
Matthew 10:22	To endure is to bear up courageously.	"All men will hate you because of me, but he who stands firm to the end will be saved." Jesus counsels his disciples as He sends them forth.	We must remember that doing God's will does not always lead to smooth sailing. The world will continue to stand against you.
Matthew 24:33	To endure is to bear up under trials. It is to have fortitude.	"but he who stands firm to the end will be saved. Jesus encourages His followers.	To endure is to know that God will rescue.
Mark 4:11	To endure is to have firm roots.	"But since they have no root, they endure only a short time. When trouble or persecution comes because of the word, they quickly fall away.	Only true believers can endure for the Gospel.

No Looking Back: Leaving the Past, Prison and Recidivism Behind

Scriptures	Definitions	Biblical Context	Application
John 6:27	To endure is to live for the Lord. To endure is to be in a state of expectancy.	Do not work for food that spoils, but for food that endures to eternal life which the Son of man will give you. On Him God the Father has placed His seal of approval.	Gain comfort from enduring distress, because we are learning how to help others.
2 Corinthians 1:6	Endurance is cheerful patient continuance.	Paul is willing to be distressed to learn to give comfort, and encouragement to others. We receive comfort and consolation because you are comforted.	Gain comfort from enduring distress, because we are learning how to help others.
Hebrews 11:27	To endure is to act in faith	By faith he left Egypt not fearing the King's anger; he persevered because he saw Him who is invisible. Moses led by faith.	Faith is needed to endure when the end is not known.

Scriptures	Definitions	Biblical Context	Application
2 Timothy 2:3	To endure is to undergo hardships, to suffer trouble, to suffer afflictions.	Paul is telling Timothy to endure the hardships like a good soldier of Christ Jesus	The believer seeks to please the Commander in Chief, Christ Jesus.
Hebrew 6:15	To endure is to be long-spirited, patient.	The writer of Hebrews reminds us of Abraham's patience. " I will surely bless you and give you many descendants. After walking patiently, Abraham received what was promised.	We must know that God's promises are true.
1 Peter 2:19	To endure is to bear up under unjust hardship.	"For it is commendable if a man bears up under the pain of unjust suffering because he is conscious of God."	God looks with favor on those who suffer for Him. This gives peace.

> Do not be anxious about anything, but in everything, by prayer and petition, with thanksgiving, present your requests to God. And the peace of God which transcends all understanding will guard your hearts and your minds in Christ Jesus.
>
> Philippians 4:6-7

A challenge to peace of mind is the propensity to worry. Worry is mental distress or agitation from concern for something impending or anticipated (Webster's, 1031). Worry can drain mental and physical resources and prevent one from handling situations effectively. Worry is not an aid to the transition passage. Worry increases stress, stops productivity and blocks enjoyment.

How can worry be stopped? As Paul stated in Philippians, the first action is prayer, presenting the cause of the worry over to God, and thanking Him for resolution. With the peace you will receive, use a problem-solving approach and apply it to the situation:

1. Assess the situation
2. Define possible solutions
3. Try what seems the best solution
4. Implement one that is workable
5. If it does not work, try the next.

One must differentiate between solvable and unsolvable problems. Ask yourself these questions:

1. Is this a present and real problem or a potential one?
2. If it is potential, how likely is it to happen?

3. If it is likely to happen, what can be done to prepare for it?
4. Is this within my control?

Unsolvable problems are things over which one has no control, and solvable problems are things over which one has some control.

One is to avoid thinking that may result in worry:

1. Do not over generalize from a single negative experience.
2. Do not make negative conclusions without adequate evidence.
3. Do not look at things with no middle ground.
4. Practice relaxation techniques.

Give every worry a limitation. Don't let a worry control you. You become mindful of what occupies your mind, choose your focus. Right focus leads to right thinking which leads to right living, which leads to staying on the freedom passage.

Philippians 4:8-9
Finally, brothers, whatever is true, whatever is noble, whatever is right, whatever is pure, whatever is lovely, whatever is admirable – if anything is excellent or praiseworthy – think about such things. Whatever you have learned or received or heard from me, or seen in me – put it into practice. And the God of peace will be with you.

Focusing on the right things will lead to right practice and a life of moral excellence. Focus on the life of those who followed Christ; their lifestyles are worth following, and receiving praise.

Go back to your moral compass and values; focus on moral purity, things worth talking about. Do not focus on dishonorable things, like lust, and permit them to control your mind. Know that the Holy Spirit controls the mind through truth. (1 John 5:6; John 17:17) Thoughts are powerful, although not seen, every thought should be in obedience to Christ. (2 Corinthians 10:5)

The transition passage to freedom is to be filled with habits, attitudes, and a lifestyle that follow from the mind which is set on virtuous things (Rydelnik, 1864).

CHAPTER 5

PRESSING TOWARD THE MARK

One must keep reaching forward toward goals that will keep them out of prison.

> Philippians 3: 12-14
> Not that I have already obtained all this, or have already been made perfect, but I press on to take hold of that which Christ Jesus took hold of me. Brothers, I do not consider myself yet to have taken hold of it. But one thing I do: Forgetting what is behind and straining toward what is ahead. I press on toward the goal to win the prize for which God has called me heavenward in Christ Jesus.

Paul is in a race of life, striving to be victorious. It is not about winning over others in a race, but about being victorious over self and following Jesus Christ. Paul is doing all in his power to win, and to *encourage* others to do the same.

> 1 Corinthians 9:25-27
> Do you not know that in a race all runners run, but only one gets the prize? Run in such a way as to get the prize. Everyone who competes in the games goes into strict training. They do it to get a crown that will not last; but we do it to get a crown that will last forever. Therefore, I do not run like a man running aimlessly; I do not fight like a man beating the air. No, I beat my body and make it my slave so that after I have preached to others, I myself will not be disqualified for the prize.

No Looking Back: Leaving the Past, Prison and Recidivism Behind

Although living in a polluted world, in order to maintain the spiritual journey of a new lifestyle, one must walk/run in a holy manner. Crime is a moral and spiritual problem and cannot be the answer to problems one meets on the road to staying free. One must break free of criminal attitudes and behaviors. This requires repentance, a change of mind and attitude. Repenting is making a decision that changes the total direction of one's life (Richards, *Encyclopedia*, 522.)

Knowing the way of righteousness, according to 2 Peter 2:21, increases the responsibility to follow it.

Remember the dog and the sow. The nature of an animal is not changed because they are cleaned on the outside. They continue to act by instincts. A converted person is changed from the inside out.

Believers need a disciplined mind. One should stay spiritually balanced knowing that Christ is coming. This gives *encouragement* for control (Wiersbe, 396). Believers live in the future tense; present actions and decisions are governed by hope in the future. Zachariah McGehee, author of *Real Strength 4 Real Men: A Path to Freedom For Those in Prison*, 2014,

Outlined pillars of strength to stay focused on the right path. These pillars are:

1. Commitment: Be committed to staying out of prison.
2. Confidence: Do not be afraid of failure, learn from them.
3. Courage: Have the courage to stand for what is right, don't fall into a herd mentality.
4. Loyalty: Have a duty to others.

5. Love: Do not be selfish.
6. Honesty: Set yourself apart from those who are not honest.
7. Humility: Put the interest of others before your own, and respect authority.
8. Kindness: Be kind with no strings attached.
9. Patience: Align expectations with needs, not wants.
10. Respect: Give Praise when praise is due.
11. Positive Influence: Be open to receiving positive influence.
12. Responsibility: Be accountable for your actions.

Building on these pillars, are seven steps for continuing in freedom.

Step 1. Be accountable:
By accepting responsibility for what is past and what is current. Changes in a person's life are internalized; the person is transformed.

Step 2: Baggage Dump:
Forgive yourself and others and move on. Do not mask pain, fear, and/or anger. Leave the past in the past. The past and future cannot co-exist.

Step 3: Develop your internal guidance system. Check your true north, morals, and values. Commit to doing the right thing.

Step 4. Know your addition(s), Acknowledge any inability to control any addition, seek help and recovery.

Step 5. Get assistance to help change thought processes.

Step 6. Learn self-acceptance and to manage your ego.

Step 7. Stop dreaming and implement your action plan.

Encouragement from mentors, friends, family, even enemies, keeps one reaching for the goal.

Pressing Toward the Mark
COME BESIDE ME

©Brenda Simuel Jackson, 2010

The economy has reduced viable income by 40%,

Need someone to come beside me!

My son has a temporary job, there were days when work lagged,

He phoned with a need you beside me, he begged!

She was fired from her job, shame prevented her from accepting the truth,

She called us, her friends, come beside me, I am almost a code blue!

Physical death has claimed several family members and friends,

Knowing they are spiritually glad and spiritually well,

Does not eliminate the occasional call, come beside me and share my sad.

Rejection is not an easy act to acknowledge, but when one comes beside to

Share the grief, the hurt is abolished.

Jesus Christ, my strength, my rock, my best friend,

Always by my side, holding me up, sustaining me, Keeping me forever by His Side.

No Looking Back: Leaving the Past, Prison and Recidivism Behind

The scorned need encouragement to continue on the journey of life, and every believer has an obligation to encourage.

Acts 9:26-27
> When he [Paul] came to Jerusalem, he tried to join the disciples, but they were all afraid of him, not believing that he really was a disciple, But Barnabas took him and brought him to the apostles. He told them how Saul on his journey had seen the Lord and that the Lord had spoken to him, how in Damascus, he had preached in the name of Jesus.

Acts 11:25-26
> Then Barnabas went to Tarsus to look for Saul. And when he found him, he brought him to Antioch. So for a whole year Barnabas and Saul met with the Church, and taught great numbers of people...

Assessment of Encouragement:

1. On your journey how often do you need to be encouraged?
2. What scriptures do you read to encourage yourself?
3. What causes you to need encouragement?
4. Are you encouraged through prayer?
5. Do you have a friend or mentor who gives you encouragement?
6. If 5 is yes, how does the person encourage you?

7. Are you an encourager?

8. How do you encourage others?

The Greek term for encourage is koinonia which means fellowship. It is sharing in common. It is communication. Another Greek term for encourage is parakaleo, meaning to call for help, to comfort, to invite, or to come to the side of. Parakaletos, is the noun, and means counselor, one who helps; one who intercedes. Obstacles in the pathway, such as, still no job, create need for encouragement. Dark places, rejection causes need for encouragement. When you are staying on the path of your future, and returning to old ways, encouragement is needed.

Remember Isaiah 41:10, "So do not fear, for I am with you; do not be dismayed, for I am your God. I will strengthen you and help you, I will uphold you with my righteous right hand.

Through encouragement, commitment is renewed, and comfort is received. Encouragement also warns of pending dangers. Encouragement aids in attaining the goal of never looking back, and reaching the mark, of continuous freedom.

Brenda M. Rudolph was an encourager to her niece, who did time twice in prison. She was to her niece as Barnabas was to Paul. One who came along side, and provided words of encouragement, when one is at their lowest. One who will come looking for you, when you are spiritually low. An encourager listens and understands the struggles. An encourager is a mentor who will guide and help one to stay focused. A mentor will counsel when needed the most. An encourager will keep one from making the mistake that robs a person of freedom, and a new life.

The angels of the Lord were with Lot and his family as they left Gomorrah, sin city. One of the angels said to Lot and his family, "Flee for your lives! Don't look back, and don't stop in the Plains, flee to the mountains… (Gen 19:17), but Lot's wife looked back, and she became a pillar of salt" (Gen 19:26). Jesus taught His disciples what not to do on His return. "…one who is on the roof of his house, with his goods inside, should not go down to get them…likewise, no one in the field should go back for anything. Remember Lot's wife! Whoever tries to keep his life will lose it, and whoever loses his life will preserve it" (Luke 17:30-33).

    The greatest encourager is Jesus The Christ. Keep your eyes attentive on Him; stay focused on God's Word. Success is yours; there is no need to turn back.

BIBLIOGRAPHY

Bibles

"Amplified Verson" in *KJV & Amplified Parallel Bible*. Grand Rapids, Michigan:Zondervan, 1987.

Berry, Pecker George. *Interlinear Greek-English New Testament. KJV*. Grand Rapids, Michigan: Baker Book House, 1987.

Aland, Barbara, et al. (Eds). *The Greek New Testament*, 4th Rev. ed. German Deutsche: Bibilgesellschaft, United Bible Societies, 1994.

Barker, Kenneth, Gen Ed. *The NIV Study Bible, New International Version*. Grand Rapids, Michigan: Zondervan Bible Publishers, 1985.

Barnes, Dr. Peter, and Deffenbough, Robert. *Layman's Bible Commentary, Acts Through2 Corinthians*. Vol. 10, USA: Barbour, 2008.

Radmacher, Earl D. Ge. Ed. *The Nelson Study Bible*. Nashville: Thomas Nelson Publishers, 1997.

Books, Articles

Arndt, William F. and Gingrich F. Wilbur. *A Greek-English Lexicon of The New Testament.*

2nd Ed. Rev. Chicago: University of Chicago Press, 1979.

Brandon, James E. *The Other Side of the Fence: How To Become an Unbound Man of God*

While and After Doing Time in Prison. E-book. January 18, 2021

Clinton, Tim Dr., and Hawkins, Ron Dr. *Biblical Counseling Quick Reference Guide*. USA: AACC Press, 2007.

Davis, Chike T. PhD., *"39 Core Values and How to Live by Them"*, Psychology Today, July 12, 2018.

Docker, David S. Gen Ed. *Holman Bible Handbook*. Nashville Tenn.: Holman Bible Publishers, 1992.

"Rules and Regulations", Federal Register, Vol 87, No 29, February 11, 2022.

McMehee, Zachariah. *Real Strength 4 Real Men: A Path to Freedom for Those in Prison.* eBook, Kindle: April 4, 2014.

Nolan, Pat. *When Prisoners Return*. USA: Prisonfellowship, 2004.

Radmacher, Earl, Allen, Ronald B., House, Wayne H. eds. *New Illustrated Bible Commentary*. Nashville: Thomas Nelson, 1999.

Rayburn, Robert Dr, Keathley, THM, Hampton J., Lester Stephen Dr., Miller, Thm, Jeffery. *Layman's Bible Commentary. Galatians through Philemon*. Vol. 11, USA: Barbour Publishing, 2008.

Richards, Lawrence O. *New International Encyclopedia of Bible Words*. Grand Rapids: Zondervan Publishing House, 1991.

_____. *The Revell Bible Dictionary*. New Jersey: Fleming H. Revell Company, 1984

_____. *The Teacher's Commentary*. Wheaton, Ill.: Victor Books, 1987.

Rydelnik, Michael and Vanlaningham, Michael. Gen Eds. *The Moody Bible Commentary*. Chicago: Moody Publishers, 2014

Bibliography

Webster's Seventh New Collegiate Dictionary. Based on Webster's third New International Dictionary G&C. Springfield, Massachusetts: Merriam Co., 1965.

Wiersbe, Warren W. *Be. Encouraged.* USA: Victor Books, 1988.

_____. *The Bible Exposition Commentary, New Testament.* Volume 11,

Ephesians – Revelation. Colorado Springs: David Cook, 1989.

_____, *Old Testament.* Joshua – Esther.

Colorado Springs: David C. Cook, 2008.

_____. The Prophets. Isaiah – Malachi. Colorado Springs: David C. Cook, 2002.

_____. Wisdom Poetry.

Job – Song of Solomon. Colorado Springs, 2004.

Internet Data

"Bureau of Justice Statistics", *Prisoners in 2020, Table 9.*

https://www.prisonpolicy.org/blog/2022/01/11/bsj_update/

Foroux, Darius. *List of 8 core Values.*
https://dariousforous.com/core-values/

https://icmt.org/articles/pm-magazine/strengthening-your-moral-compass-overcome=ethical-roadblocks.

https://virtuefirst.info/virtues/responsibility/

https://www.aconsciousrethink.com/8562/take-responsibility.

https://www.ethicssage.com/2018/06/set-your-moral-compass-TrueNorthhtlm

https://letterpile.com/personal-essays/raping-THE-CAUSES-AND-THE-CONSEQUENCES7/8/2020

Mindfulness – Muse, *Choose to Live According to Your True Values.* https://www.mindfulness.com/

Nam, Sooji. *Get out of That place: Former S C Inmate says reentry program changed his life.*

https://wpda.com/news/local/helping-you-get-out-of-that-place-former-inmate-says-reentry-programs-changed-his-life.

Northwestern University Information Technology. *Project Framework Planning: Transition,11-2-2020.* https://info.gov/tjc/module-7-section-2-transition-plan-content.

Pew Research Center. https://www.pewforum.org/religious-landscape-study/state/michigan/Retrieved 3/11/2021.

The 10 most Important Human Values, Inspirational Speech. https://Iamfearlesssoul.com/

What's The Difference Between Ethics, Morals, and Values.

https://examples.yourdictionary.com/differencebetween-ethics-morals-andvalues.html

worldpopulationreview.com/state-rankings/recidivism-rates-by-state. Retrieved June 1, 2022.

Bibliography

www.heartsspiritmind.com/personal-growth/what-is-a-moralcompass/

Zitzman, Bryan, Ph.D, LMFT.
https://www.beliefnet.com/inspirationalmoral-compass.AXPX. Retrieved 4/22/2020.

_____. *Ex-Offenders Resource Guide.*
http://www.hard2hire.com/Ex_offenders. Retrieved 8/17/2022.

Interviews and Public Addresses

Brandon, James, Graduation Address, Federal Correctional Institution, Milan, Michigan 28, June, 2022.

Edmonds, Tracey. Personal Interview. 14, July, 2022.

Geddes, Trevis. Personal Interview, 20, April, 2022.

McHaley, Rochell. Personal Interview. 27, August, 2022.

Rudolph, Brenda M. Personal Interview. 20, August 2022.

APPENDIX

MICHIGAN RE-ENTRY RESOURCES
FOR RETURNING CITIZENS

I. Parolee Resources
   A. Crossroads – Main Office
      2424 W. Grand Blvd, Detroit, MI 48204
      https://crossroadsofmichigan.org
      1. Outreach Agency
      2. Emergency Assistance
      3. Counseling
      4. Emergency Food
      5. Emergency Clothing
      6. One –time Prescription
      7. Employment
      8. Transportation
      9. Obtaining Identification
   B. Medical Assistance – Hope Medical Clinic
      https://thehopeclinic.org
      1. Hope Clinic, P.O. Box 980311, Ypsilanti, MI 48198-0311
      2. Hope Medical & Dental, 518 Harriet, Ypsilanti, MI 48198
      3. Hope Wayne Medical Clinic, 33608 Palmer, Westland, MI, 734-710-6688
      4. mnitkiiwicz@thehopeclinic.org
   C. Expungement Process:
      1. Project Clean Slate
         a. Judges can expunge person's criminal record.
         b. Expunge up to three minor offenses

2. Lakeshore Legal Aid Counsel & Advocacy Law Live, 248-443-8068 16250 Northland Dr. Suite 363, Southfield, MI 48075
    a. New Client Intake: 888-783-8190
    b. Sets aside an adult criminal conviction
    c. Sets aside a juvenile adjudication
    d. Driver's license restoration
3. Federal Civil Pro Bono Project, 313-961-6120 https://www.detroitlawyer.org dba@detroitlawyer.org 645 Griswold, Suite1356, Detroit, MI 48226
4. Detroit Legal Service Clinic, 313 961-6120 Ext. 206 Penobscot Building, 13th floor, Smart Detroit Conference Rooms, 645 Griswold, Detroit, MI 48226 https://www.detroitlawyer.org/clinic

D. Free Tattoo Removal, www.dhdc1.org
  1. Freedom Ink
  2. Detroit Hispanic Corp., 1211 Trumbull, Detroit, MI 48216

E. Mental Health/Substance Abuse Treatment Program
  1. www.comcareserv.org 313-976-4880
  2. Community Care Service Admin., 26184 W. Outer Drive, Lincoln Park, MI 48146
  3. Catholic Social Services of Washtenaw County, 734-971-9781 CCSW Main Building, 4925 Packard, Ann Arbor, MI 48109 https://csswashtenaw.org/bhs/offender-success

F. Aid for Going Back to Job Training and to Work
  1. Here to Help Foundation HeretohelpFoundation@cloud.com P.O. Box 480, Royal Oak, MI 48068

Appendix

https://www.heretohelpFoundation.org/active/Returning-hope-to-returning-citizensC32
   a. Furniture
   b. 1 month's rent or security deposit
2. Goodwill Industries of Greater Detroit, 313-557-4834 https://goodwilldetroit.org/services/for-individuals 3111 Grand River Ave., Detroit, MI 48208
   a. Employment Development Services
   b. Transitional work experience
   c. Academic Training
   d. Job placement
   e. Employment follow up
3. S.H.A.R, 313-894-8276, 313-834-8444 Ext.2208, 313-894-8208
   http://sharine.org/index.html/#home
   1852 W. Grand Blvd., Detroit, MI 48208
   a. Ambulatory detoxification
   b. Residential Substance Abuse treatment
   c. Outpatient programs
   d. Transitional housing
   e. Recovery support
   f. Prevention services

G. Tax Incentives and Work Credit Incentives for Employers to hire Returning Citizens
   1. Michigan Fidelity Bonding Program
      https://www.michigan.gov/leo/o58637.33691422_64361_525309-00.html
   2. Michigan Bureau of Workers & =Unemployment Compensation, 313-456-2105
      https://www.mitalent.org/employer-other-resources
      WOTC Unit, Cadillac Place, 3024 W. Grand Blvd., Suite 11-450, Detroit, MI, 48202

H. Employment Opportunities
1. Center for Employment Opportunities, 313-400-0024, 7310 Woodward Ave., Suite 701B, Detroit, MI 40202 https://ceoworks.org/impact-evidence
2. Live Rite Resource Center, 586-217-5899 27700 Gratiot, Roseville, MI 48066, Liveritestructuredcorp@gmail.com https://www.liveritestructured.corp.com
3. Staffing Agencies
    a. Advanced Staffing resumes to: Resumes@advancedstaffingonline.com Contact: Gene Fax: 734-943-6094
    b. Arcadia Staff Resources Contact: Marge 248-477-0900
    c. Express Employment Professionals Call for an Interview, 248-474-5000
    d. Kelly Services (Felony must be 7 years old) Contact person: Denise 313-967-9355
    e. Labor Ready Incorporated, 313-446-9675 or 313-383-4600
    f. Minute Men Staffing Contact Person: Julie 313-849-3555
    g. Phoenix Personnel 586-275-2986 or 734-284-2121
4. Job Assistance Programs
    a. Cass Community Social Services, 313-883-2277 http://casscommunity.org/ 11745 Rosa Parks Blvd, Detroit, MI 48206
    b. Central City Integrated Health, www.centralcityhealth.com

Appendix

10 Peterboro St., Detroit, 48203, 313-831-3160
    aa. Job training/placement
    bb. Counseling Services, Housing Assistance

c. Goodwill Industries of Greater Detroit
http://shopgoodwilldetroit.com/locations/
4 store locations in Wayne County

d. Jewish Vocational Services (JVS), http://www.jvsdet.org
Arnold E. Frank Building, 4250 Woodward Ave, Detroit, 48201
    aa. Gap program – provides employment services for homeless
    bb. Job Training

e. Michigan Works, 800-285-9675
http://wwwmichiganworks.org/job-seekers/ Visit location to register and access job services
    aa. 18100 Meyers, Detroit, 313-873-7321
    bb. 9301 Michigan Ave., Detroit, 313-962-9675
    cc. 555Connor Street 1st floor, Detroit, 313-579-4825

I. Training Opportunities
1. Cambridge Computer Institute, 248-589-1078, 21700 Greenfield Road, Oak Park, MI 48237
2. Carnegie Institute, 248-589-1078
550 Stephensen Highway, Troy, MI 48083
3. Career Quest Learning Center – Lansing
3215 South Pennsylvania Avenue, Lansing, MI 48910

4. Dorsey School of Business
   31739 John R. Road, Madison Heights, MI 48071
5. Dorsey School of Business, 586-296-3225
   31542 Gratiot Ave, Roseville, MI 48066
6. Focus Hope Machinist Training Institute, 313-494-4560
   1400 Oakman Blvd, Detroit, MI 48238
7. MIAT College of Technology, 734-423-2100
   2955 South Haggerty Road, Canton, MI 48188
8. New Horizons of MI, 734-434-7320
   14115 Farmington Road, Livonia, MI 48154

J. Internet sources for job postings
   1. Simplyhired
      http://www.simplyhired.com/search?qfelony&l=Detroit%2c+mi&job=Lod15BqYs42mcs1eTy+cz-rGOQbdUzsJyrKD2UVnvi034fopq
   2. Ziprecruiters
      http://www.ziprecruiter.com/jobs/felony-friendly-in-michigan
   3. Jobs for Felons – Updated Daily
      http://www.jobsforfelonshub.com/stytos/jobs-for-felons-in-michigan
   4. Indeed
      http://www.indeed.com/q-felony-friendly-l-Michigan=jobs.html

II. Housing
   A. Michigan Housing Authority
      http://www.jobsforfelonshub.com/housing-for-felons/Michigan/
      1. Michigan Apartment Listings on Craigslist
      2. Reentry Programs

Appendix

    3. Michigan Religious Community
- B. Apartments.com
  http://www,yellowpages.com/detroit-mi/felon-friendly-apartments

III. Religious Composition of Adults in Michigan (Pew Research Center)
- A. "Christian Faiths" 70%
  1. Evangelical Protestant 25%
  2. Mainline Protestant 18%
  3. Historically Black Protestant 8%
  4. Catholic 18%
  5. Mormon <1%
  6. Orthodox Christian <1%
  7. Jehovah's Witness 1%
  8. Other Christian 1%
- B. Non-Christian Faiths 5%
  1. Jewish 1%
  2. Muslim 1%
  3. Buddhist 1%
  4. Hindu <1%
- C. Other World Religions <1%

ABOUT THE AUTHOR

Minister Brenda Simuel Jackson, (BA, MA, Master of Divinity, Ph.D.) is a born again Christian, affiliated with the Baptist Denomination. She is a member and Minister of New Prospect Missionary Baptist Church, and does ministry through BSJ Christian Seminars, Inc., a 501(c)3 Prison/Jail Ministry. She is a graduate of Wayne State University, Moody Theological Seminary – Michigan, formerly Michigan Theological Seminary, and Jacksonville Theological Seminary.

Dr. Jackson has over thirty years of professional experience in human services, education administration, and management, as well as part-time collegiate instruction. She is currently the Transition Coach at The Federal Correctional Institution in Milan Michigan where she continues to teach classes and adjunct faculty member of Owens Community College, Ohio.

Dr. Jackson is a published writer. Her eighth book, Prayers from Prison, was completed in 2019.

Dr. Jackson also hosted a radio broadcast, "God's Teaching Moments". Her Christian Journey includes short term outreach mission and prison ministry assignments in Japan, South Africa, Jamaica, Ghana, Zambia, Swaziland, Botswana, and Kenya.

Dr. Jackson is a called minister of the Gospel. She was ordained in the Gospel ministry November 30, 2018, New Prospect

Missionary Baptist Church. She was licensed as a minister of the Gospel November 13, 2005 and is a Chaplain with the National Baptist Convention, USA and the International Association of Chaplains. Her vineyard is the prisons of the world.

www.ingramcontent.com/pod-product-compliance
Lightning Source LLC
Chambersburg PA
CBHW052122110526
44592CB00013B/1714